Love... everything else is... & our problem...

BE
UNDUMPABLE

It Starts with You

Be Unumpable

By Paul Posey

It Starts with You

Contact Me

Please follow me:

Website:

N2PGA.ORG

Facebook:

Paul Posey

Instagram:

Neg_2_Pos

Twitter:

@mrneg2pos

Available for:

Public Speaking Events

Family Workshops

event contact me at:

http://www.n2pga.org/contact-us.html

Preface

We spend so much of our single life looking for "The One." Since there is no perfect science to finding the perfect partner, we are forced to find a loving partner through a lot of trial and error. But all our trials are pretty much the same, yet we never take a systematic look at how we go from being single to marriage. I have been a boyfriend, a husband, a single husband* and even the transition man. Each position showed me a different angle of what many are going through.

Time and a lot of errors have forced me to open my eyes and pay attention to the process we go through to find a mate. I was tired of getting it wrong like many who are still out there searching. I started looking at the search process we use to finding someone and formed it into something that might help someone to see if the next person they meet is for them. We subconsciously generate a list of must-haves; which are things that we want our mate to possess to show that we are evenly yoked. In this part of the search, it seems we are asking a lot of the next person. In order to capture the attention of a person to go through the process of starting a relationship we must be willing to possess certain tangible items and intangible traits to let the other person know you are worthy of their time and capable sustaining a long-term relationship as well. If you want to have the best chance at being in a long-term relationship you must make yourself "Undumpable."

My Disclaimer:

I have spent a good portion of my adult life watching people as a hobby. I am writing this book to share some of the things I have seen and expose how we as human beings struggle to find that imperfect mate. By no means am I attempting to take away from your belief that God will send you "The One." "However comma" that person was probably already sent to you, but you didn't like the wrapper.

Table of Content

<u>Volume One</u>

Be Undumpable

What is Undumpable?

First, let me say there is no need to google it, there is no such word. But let me be the first to coin the phrase, "be undumpable." I came up with this word after many failed attempts to being in a stable and loving relationship. There were things I could and should have done on my part to be properly prepared to be in a relationship and marriage. Undumpable means that you have taken steps to having your life in order before seeking a commitment with someone you think and feel has everything you need to be in a relationship. A self-inventory should be taken before you generate your list of non-negotiables and must haves that you may think the other person must possess. You must have basic partnership skills to complement the partner that you are seeking. If we all lived our lives seeking to be the best partners while we are single, we would have fewer divorces and break-ups.

We have heard the old cliché that says, "a good woman/man is hard to find," this becomes irrelevant if you find someone and you are not in a position to keep them. Some of you may shake your head at the idea, but by the time you are done reading this volume, you will say hmmm, he might have something there.

How to Be Undumpable?

You should be in the business of doing self-reflection to see what you can improve within yourself to be a better partner. I have taken upon myself to improve on a few things I felt hurt me in previous relationships.

To include:

- Being a better listener. I improved this trait by watching YouTube classes on being a listener.
- Learning to budget money in a manner that I could take care of a family, not just me. I bought a book on curing debt and created a budget form to monitor my money.
- Learn to express my feelings instead of bottling them up inside to later come out as an emotional explosion.
- No arguing rule, there is no such thing that every couple argues, people who like to argue say that.
- Help my partner grow, not just exist, but help them be the best they can be.

"Your life is but wet clay, and you get to mold it." N2P

There is no magic to being undumpable. If you are reading this book, at some point in your life you have been dumped or cheated on. Have you evaluated why did this happen? The lowest part of my life was failing in my marriage. I was totally ill prepared to be a husband and take on a family. Another cliché, "I did the best with what I had," is the national anthem for failures. We all had practiced driving and parking before we got our driver's license. We all were so thrilled to have the freedom of driving and even more eager to show our driver's license to all who could stand to look at the picture. Why don't we do this for our relationships? Either it was not taught to us, or we were not lucky enough to have had it modeled for us as children. Nevertheless, that is not a reason to ruin someone else's life as you learn as you go.

You also need to remember each time you were dumped in a relationship. Then remember why you have dumped others. It is ok to recall why your friends and family members either got dumped or had to dump others as well. Some of the reason need not be repeated if you can help it. I know for a fact I can list at least five reasons:

1. Lack of steady employment
2. Drug usage
3. Cheating
4. Old baggage
5. Financial burden

Each item listed above has a reason or story behind it. Let's take the reason, a person having issues of maintaining steady employment. Two adults may need to pool their resources in a relationship to makes sure all bills are being paid to have a place to call home. If one of the partners feels a need to walk away from a job because they felt it was beneath them and has repeated this cycle a few times. I would deem this as a "relationship violation" which could be grounds to be dumped.

If I had this issue maintaining a job, I would be seeking a job that is made for me, while I still have a job. This issue should have been addressed while single, not a learning lesson while in a relationship. It is not fair to other person to function in this cycle while someone is depending on you.

A person who has some type of addiction is asking their partner to accept this behavior as a normal part of the relationship. We all know over time this will hurt, even ruin a relationship. If you have a substance issue, you are very dumpable and should seek help before you take on a relationship.

Just because you have not seen this type of self-growth does not mean it cannot be done. The question is how bad you want a peaceful and loving relationship? You must prepare yourself to be the best partner in order to sustain your long-term relationship, it really helps to do this before you meet "The One."

Why Be Undumpable?

It is easy to say the reason you should be undumpable, is to be in a loving relationship and live happily ever after. There is one bigger reason and far more important.

"If you are ready, it exposes the un-ready."
N2P

The work you do on yourself is your protector. It will clearly expose those who are not ready to be in a committed relationship. If so, they would have completed the work just like you have.

If you are near the age of 50 right now, you see this in your daily search. People who are not ready to move forward are suitors who are still trying to find a place to live. They have not invested in their retirement, which is a flag at the door. When you must make special concessions to have someone in your life, you are the one taking the risk. At the end of the day, they were okay with their life status and their flags.

It is your right to show what you bring to the table because you earned all your failures and scrapes and are willing to make a better life for yourself in preparation to be in a relationship. When you do not strive to be a better partner, you are clearly putting yourself at the mercy of the other person to accept you and your flaws. I would call that being "Relationship Thirsty."

Relationship thirsty is when you have many missing pieces to your life. You are lunging towards a person to be in their life for something other than love. Whether it is a place to live or financial gain. Either way, most of the work that needs to be done has not been done for one reason or another. I do not knock the thirsty game, because some people feel they need to be needed in their relationship while others are very content being taken care of.

You should also be undumpable just in case you do not find the one. This will put you in the position where you do not have to worry about sustaining your own life. This is your own world of functional peace. It drastically lowers that feeling of thirst to be a relationship and makes you feel safe at the same time.

Undumpable Vs. Perfection

Each time I speak on this topic, someone likes to throw out the fallback statement, "no one is perfect." It is often used to counter any thought that self-improvement, personal reliability, and responsibility, when it comes to relationships with other people. After many years of working and saving money for retirement, monitoring your credit score, and creating the buying power to be able to get what you want when you want it is what we all should be striving for. Not always being forced to put love on lay-a-way.

I'm sorry, I am no longer in the business of functioning on 6-cylinders when I am an 8-cylinder engine when it comes to relationships. For the Ladies, why would you want to pay full price for something that you know is a knock-off.

When I started this book, the full thought was to help people to understand how preparation helps, not to seek perfection. If you have a bag full of flaws and you are selling damage goods with many missing pieces, you are wrong. We should not be afraid to say this aloud. Some will do whatever it takes to fool potential mates only to let them down later. To those who accepts these flaws and conditions; you have little room to complain because you were not vigilant in your process in searching for the best mate. At the end of the day, people are seeking acceptance of their imperfections.

Nowhere it says that you cannot work on your relationship short comings to overcome your past failures before entering the loving phase of your next relationship. The key is not be side tracked by things that could have been avoided from the start.

Everything should start with you, but we are not made like that. We are using our eyes, trends, fads, looks and our heart to find "The One." The there are things we need to secure within our own lives first. When it comes to making a better choice for love, a solid base line in the beginning would give our hearts a fighting chance at a long term loving relationship.

Next Up:

Making a Better Choice for Love

Volume Two

Making a Better Choice for Love

Selection Process

There comes a time in our life, where we come to an understanding of what we need and want in a mate. We all want love, but that is not the issue here. There must be a way to protect our love and feelings from being destroyed time and time again. We could go with, "love at first sight," which is a visual adornment linked to an emotional response to a person you do not even know. It is where our eyes have sent a text message to the brain and said, "I have found the one." The down side to that is we have no clue if this person can receive love or even worse can give love. Love, at first sight, does not always work, but it is truly a blessing when it does.

Some of the key elements to picking the best mate for you is to possess a list of must haves, non-negotiables, and a person who is capable of being open enough to be explored. There are hundreds of people you can see in passing during your day to day travels to and from work, but maybe only one could be an earnest match for you. The selection process consists of knowing the physical characteristics you want in your partner. I know what you are thinking, looks aren't everything. But I'm sure there have been many in your past that were too short, too tall, too wide, and too hairy people out there trying to get your attention. Hence, you immediately saw something in their physical presence that was not appealing to you.

*If you are the type of person who feels looks mean nothing, please skip down to the Vetting Process chapter.

You should know what your type is. Do you like tall, short, bald, or toothless people? This is your personal list of "likes" that you physically desire in a mate. I say this because we are visual creatures, this goes for men and women. We are often drawn to people physically before we even know if they can speak a full sentence. That is the nature of the beast in us, and it is very rare that we move away from this instinctive search. Even Ray Charles had a method of choosing a woman.

When we select mates that are not visually pleasing to us, we seek to change the things we do not like about them later in the relationship. Whether it's the clothes they wear or the few pounds you want them to shed, all the way up to their fake hair. This is right in line where people say, "accept me as I am." Your list of physical attributes is important in your search, and you can refine it, bend it, and give it exceptions to your rules. The bottom line is, what you accept in your life is what you will have. You might as well get it right from the start before you commit to someone you might lose later while attempting to force change on them. Only chase or invite those in your life that you want to wake up and see every day for the rest of your life.

Generating your list is important, and you should be real with yourself in doing so. To include the following:

1. Height- My height or shorter

2. Weight- Less than me

3. Hair – Short, to Locks,

4. Teeth- No gold

5. Style of Dress- dressed for the occasion

6. Jewelry- none moderate

7. Shoes- flats to heels

8. Make up- none to moderate

The list I have shared comes from what I find that standout to me when meeting a woman for the first time. These are commonalities in the attributes amongst the women I have been physically attractive in my past. I have tried to accept physical attributes that are outside of what I like, but deep down inside I know I would want them to change something to be pleasing to my eye. Instead of forcing my visual will on a woman, I'd rather not settle. Look at your trends and make your list of attributes you like. A realistic list of what you have found attractive is important and a great place to start.

Yes, you are correct skin stretches and looks fade, but this is how we are made up, and most people still go by what they see. We like what we like, and we tend to stick with it. This is one of the ways we judge who will be in our life. Love will keep you, but it is not love that attracts you.

Unrealistic Expectations

The unrealistic physical expectations are illogical things that tend to keep people single. This is displayed in a few different ways in the quest for a relationship and should be addressed.

When people are seeking an unrealistic attribute, which is something that they cannot complement in their partner.

Health is very important to a relationship. If you want me to love you until we are old and gray; my partner needs to have a healthy agenda. Smoking cigarettes, excessive drinking, and a daily intake of greasy foods are not in line with that. If you want to be with a person who is practicing a healthy lifestyle, you will have to adopt that lifestyle for the sake of peace and longevity.

The same could be said when it comes to having children or not to have children. Some people are still dreaming of being a new parent and want to start a family. The other parent's child raising days may have already ended. This relationship is starting off on the wrong foot for sure because one person is trying to change the mind of the other.

When people are not evenly yoked...

Pursuing an extrovert and you are an introvert, this is not a complimentary match. Extroverts have a need to communicate on many levels and are very outgoing. If they feel the need to get their communication groove on and are out in the public eye, you may not want to entertain them. This may force the extrovert to seek someone who will communicate with them, not just sit, and listen.

Financial goals are just as important. Not so much as your history of failing financially, but what are you doing to correct those shortcomings. If you have a credit score of 475 and the person you are pursuing is topping out at 800; at 475 your bounce back plan must be impressive and functional. If not, you are a financial hazard to them, by not showing potential for growth.

Of course, you could argue this, but if you have paid all your bills for years and had a retirement plan in place, and the person you are interested in has not. The question in the back of your head should be, "do they need me?" or "do they want me?"

Non-negotiables

Knowing what your non-negotiables are and why they made your list is very important. The list may consist of things you have found that may be damaging to the idea of a long-term relationship.

For example:

1. Drug usage

2. Lack of income

3. Lack of professional goals

4. Inadequate housing

5. No transportation

6. Criminal record (for acts of violent)

7. Anger issues

8. Negative attitude

9. Does not understand the value of time

10. Poor Communication Skills

I have my personal reasons for each item on my list. You will have your reasons as well and why they made your list. What is on your list??

"You have what you accept" N2P

Vetting Process

The Vetting Process is based on you finding out if the person you chose possesses any of those items on your non-negotiable list. I meet people often who have accepted one or two of their non-negotiables in their life only to regret it later in a failed relationship. You must know yourself and be clear about what you want. If not, you have failed yourself and the person who has assumed you accepted something about them which is on your non-negotiable list. Best thing to do is share your list early and stand by it or forever hold your tongue.

Watching a person in action as they conduct their life is important. How they function with their money, friends, family, and their job should be a part of the process. If they have children, does the child or children admire them? Are they conscious of time? What is their religious belief? Do they enjoy using drugs?

You are vetting the whole person because it is your goal to have them in your life in a long-term relationship.

What if we knew all of this before going out on a date? Would you change your mind about moving forward? Or would you dismiss those things for the sake of the potential of a loving relationship? These are the things you must ask yourself and only you can give the answer.

We are so tired, hurt, and frustrated that we try to date and pursue a relationship like it's going out of style? We cannot rush the process because it only makes things messy later.

For example:

You meet someone, and you go out with them a few times. You find out a month later they smoke cigarettes. Cigarettes are on your non-negotiable list. They have been hiding the fact they smoke the whole time. Now you must make a choice.

    A. You ask them to quit

    B. You start smoking too

    C. You stop dating them

    D. You try to compromise with them because they are a great person

Most smokers want you to accept their smoking with a promise to quit later. Now you are forced to make an emotional decision. You are asking yourself, "am I willing to compromise with their smoking?" Yes, this decision does stink (no pun intended), but they are hoping you chose "D." Once you accept this behavior there is no wiggling out of it the other person's eyes.

No one is perfect, but that is no excuse to accepting things you feel that are not right for you.

The Time Factor

The most precious thing we have from our birth to our last second on earth is time. We cannot get one second back. Once you truly understand this concept, it could change your whole view of on how to find a mate. Have you noticed there had been a consistency in the amount of time it takes to vet a person in respect to the idea of either wanting to end the courtship or move it forward? I have, and this is what I have seen time and time again.

Time frames

Day 1 - This is the visual stimulation phase. You see the person, you speak and exchange information.

Day 2 to Day 14 – The question and answer phase begin. This is where you share your likes, dislikes, and non-negotiables. You get an understanding of the other person's work schedule and solid commitments, which could be church, children, hobbies, and working out, etc.

Day15 to Day 30- If you find that you are compatible with the information shared up to this point; it would be safe to say that a light get together is in order. **Note*** I would not allow someone to drag this out beyond 30 days. (time wasters)

Day 31 to Day 89- You should never assume anyone is 100% single. You are in an elimination competition phase. You are in competition with their past relationships, pains, and fears, as well as someone else who wants to be in their life. You will get to see how they are with their finances, work relationships, interaction with friends and family. You should know where they are living to include whether they are buying or renting and what their plans are for housing in the future. Are they in a job or career? Does the person have future professional goals?

Day 90 to 120 – By this time you should know whether they have significant potential to be in a relationship with you. However, this not an automatic relationship starting point. Before you let your heart run amuck and start making plans, you must make sure they are ready to move forward into a relationship. The person is fully engaged, you both have created a basic schedule and have open communication to discuss any and everything.

Day 121 to 180- You are in relationship mode. Your lives are beginning to merge; schedules are beginning to work together. You are comfortable in each other's space and the only thing left is "the talk."

The Talk is a verbal communication that you and partner are entering a committed relationship. One should not assume the other person is feeling the same way about the last six months. Being on the same page is paramount to moving forward. Up to this point, you have held off on making relationship goals, sharing keys and critical information about your financial institutes. Now you may release a sigh of relief because you are finally in a real relationship. Anything before 180 days, I think you are setting yourself for failure once again.

Selecting and Vetting are just at the tip of the iceberg. There are so many layers that must be peeled back before being in a secure relationship moving toward marriage. We often skip many of those layers in the pursuit of love. We just want to love and be loved. When you move too fast, you fail, and you tend to have signs of buyer's remorse. Anger, unexpected arguments, loss of sexual appetite, and the feeling you have wasted your time. Time is the one thing we cannot afford to waste. Sure, you may say, what does this guy know. Well, I just started paying attention, how about you?

Next Up:

Flags and Whistles

Volume Three

Flags and Whistles

Flags

What are flags? Flags are signs that a potential mate has shown you that may not be good in your relationship. To keep this simple, we will say that there are two types of colored flags that we deal with when it comes to evaluating a potential love interest. You have your yellow flag; it consists of things that can be worked out with minor adjustments to improve themselves or their situation to be a good mate for you.

Examples of Yellow Flags:

- Slight issues with finances
- Temporay housing situation
- In between jobs (fully employable)
- Going through a divorce
- Children
- Not ready for commitment

Let's take a look at what makes a yellow flag...

Having your finances in order is important in your own life. When it comes to accepting someone else in your life for a long-term relationship, you must be sure their finances are not a burden to your long-term relationship and financial goals. A person that has blemishes on their credit is not a bad candidate. It is what they are doing about their financial issue that makes a difference. A person could be taking a course on getting out of debt, sending letters to debtors and setting up a realistic budget.

If a person shares that they are having financial hardships from the beginning and they have not attempted to resolve their issue, then you must make a judgement call whether to leave them where they are or help. This is why I said this type of situation is a "Yellow Flag." When a person shares something that can be fixed by way of education or motivation, it doesn't mean you cannot move forward with them, but definitely proceed with caution. "However comma" if they refuse help or have not moved in the direction to resolve the issue in a reasonable amount of time; then "Houston we have a problem," and we must raise the "red flag".

A Red Flag is a trait, characteristic, circumstance, or situation that would require extreme toleration in the context of a relationship with a person. When you accept a red flag, then you are solely responsible for your decision to move forward with this person.

Examples of Red Flags:

Criminal background in domestic violence

Suspended or revoked license

Living arrangements illogical

No job (unemployable)

Active addiction

Anger Issues

No money

Does or does not want children

Legally separated/ married

The items listed above are Red Flags, Why? Because they have a high rate of negative success in a relationship. It is unhealthy to take on the task to fix people to be in a relationship. These types of flags will require you to put an excessive amount of time and effort to find a stable foundation to be in a functional relationship.

Do not confuse this with the cliché; "You have to meet people where they are." Because when you meet people that have red flags, it means leave them right where they are.

We cannot fix people, and it doesn't matter how much potential they have, it must be in action when you meet them.

"He who has potential and does not utilize said potential has no potential" N2P

Love should not trump common sense in the early stages of meeting someone. Because no one wants to take that long boat ride down the river of regret. Of course, the other person is grateful for your acceptance of their flags and may even appreciate it, in the beginning.

Quite often people will not share these red flags at the meet and greet stage. These are often things you pick up in conversation later or via some request for help later. The full story is always weeks away when they can no longer hide their flag from you.

People who possess red flags often drown you with attention to keeping that euphoric feeling going. They won't give you a chance to breathe to make it hard to see those flaws. In their hopes, they want you emotionally invested as soon as possible to warrant your help or acceptance of the flag.

Great Example: Bouncing Tyrone is that guy who meets a woman to have a place to stay. He has worn out his welcome at his current place and knows his time is just about up. He smothers you with a lot of attention and great sex, but he is using that bargaining stick to make sure he has a place to live. Not long after he is comfortable in your home, you will see the true person. Then his house of cards begins to crumble. Needless to say, he begins his search for a new victim to take him in.

Or Rent time Rita, she does everything you like, there is no limit to her submissiveness and acrobatic sex. Things are going great until rent time. For some unforeseen reason, she is short on her rent. Now you must weigh your emotion commitment to those things she does so well. Also, you are wondering how she paid last month's rent and how is she going to pay the next month's rent as well.

I'm sure many of you have seen these types before or they are at one of your friends or family member's house right now. Bottom line people that have red flags know before they meet you. Even if they are honest about their flags, they should not get a pass. Once you accept them, they will make you suffer for waking up from the spell they casted on you.

Why Do We Bypass Flags??

There are times we go right pass flags and jump into relationships and even marriages. I think if you are over the age of 35 you have started to notice this pattern. This is because our heart wants to love. The heart is not designed to investigate or evaluate people. We have needs and a yearning to project love and often it is projected towards the wrong people. First, having a natural attraction to a person one thing. Second, our emotional needs may be at a low. When we are alone/single, we begin to miss certain things that a relationship brings to the table. Companionship and closeness are two of the main reasons that often push us out there. Besides going to work and visiting family, a single person can go weeks even months without cuddling and much needed hugs. This is why some people choose to have a pet. The pet wants to be love and held, and the person does too.

This lack of personal attention is a factor to bypassing flags. This is where you have love overshadowing logic. A person will choose a potential mate on how they feel about them and then later evaluate whether they are capable of being in a long-term relationship. Do not be a shame; this is a normal part of trial and error for love. It's just that we tend to think that love conquers all. "However comma" that does not work in adult relationships. I think the divorce stats is one way to measure that. Second, the fact most of you readers have experienced this time and time again by having those 90 day relationships.

Flags are there for a reason, to show others that this person has not completed some of the cardinal steps to being undumpable; which are clearly time wasters and will repeat this cycle until you get tired of getting it wrong.

Flags and Whistles

Whistles

Whistles are the good things we like about a person, and they tend to go off when we hear something that we find pleasing, or it is something that the person possess that we need.

Example:

Most women do not have a mechanic in their family. They often feel that they are getting ripped off when they take their vehicle to a person to fix a headlight, but ends up buying frequency grease for their radio or those new run flat windshield wipers.

Note* there are no such things as run flat windshield wipers and frequency grease.

Men often lack someone taking care them, and when they hear that a woman loves to cook, their mental whistles goes off as well.

Whistles are great, and people should share their whistle material to let a person know what they bring to the table. By sharing whistles creates a foundation that can be measured by the person's action in the future. If they say they can work on cars, you will have a reasonable assumption that if you had a car issue they could at least give some guidance to a resolution to the problem.

Some of their whistles should match or easily merge with your long-term personal or professional goals. By no means should you plan your life around another person's whistles, but it is fair to say they could be a bonus to your goals in life.

Flags and whistles go hand in hand; they simply point out things to avoid and look forward to in the future of getting to know someone. Remember, people will say and do almost anything for love; even when it comes down to hiding their flags as long as they can to get a person emotionally invested.

Next Up

Relationship IQ

Volume Four

Relationship IQ

Preface

It has been written that relationships go back as far as the conception of the earth, the moon, and stars. Today we are striving to find many things like financial freedom, peace, and love. We all have different views on how to obtain everything in a systematic way except for love. Love means something different to everyone, and no one shows love the same way as well. At this day in time, we are getting pretty close to working out most of the bugs in finding the best candidate for that loving relationship we hear or read about in books. What we don't seem to grasp is that it is a work in progress, and it would help if we came up with a solid process. We have been doing things too long to keep getting it wrong. Wrong is repeated the same fail attempts with the wrong person and expecting better results. Each relationship (should) bring us closer to a better understanding of why things work and do not work in relationships. I call this our Relationship IQ.

How do We learn?

For many years, we have used the old trial and error method. This method requires a lot of skins and tears. I like to call it the "Ole crash and burn," which seems to be the methods of choice for many.

Because we have different definitions of love, we tend to think our relationships are unique. After watching people stumble around for years, including myself, I have come to an understanding that all relationships are the same. It is sad at this age in time we are still using this old method to figure out what is a good, bad, and great relationship. We are pretty good at recording and retaining historical events, old paintings, pyramids, and event precious stones. "However comma" we are bad at retaining our simple concepts of family love and relationship love. Individually we are still learning through the art of pain and really do not have to. People are writing things down, yet we as the reader feel they are not talking to us. We still think our journey for love is unique, but in real life, only the wording of our definition of love is unique.

We seem to know better only after another failed attempt to a relationship. When you are in a relationship, and you start to notice that it is not going as you expected and you find yourself in a commitment that is truly not emotionally healthy for you. It seems that everything could go wrong, does go wrong. Instead of leaving the relationship we tend to hang in there until the end; which often ends in someone going to going jail, even worse a child is born and you have to share it with someone you thought you knew or barely knew at all.

Then you have the "give it all you got love." Where you think if you try real hard with your limited Relationship IQ, that love will conquer all. Often this pure projection of love does not result in a lasting relationship. We feel as if the person has been placed in our lives to suck the goodness out of us.

The "you ain't going to do me like the last person" is next. Where we become insecure and overbearing in a relationship, we pretty much drive people away. The pains from the previous tries tend to be guidelines to our quest for love.

We tend to move to the "acceptance phase of relationships," where most of us stop seeking the "happy ever after love" and accept the person who is loving us. It is at the point where many of us get married. Here you have the feeling that no is perfect and you are tired of the "learn as you go" school of relationships.

Have you seen these patterns before? I'm sure many of you are shaking your head saying, "he don't know me ..lol" Those steps are nothing new and most of us have been there before. Some have gone there with multiple people and some with one person over a long period of time.

We are letting our history be our teacher. I truly get it because this is the natural learning cycle of human beings. Putting our hand in fire and water is a natural part of life. We teach our children the same way in the beginning.

Here lies the problem, since the invention of the wheel we have created inventions, processes, and major theories. We have gone to the moon and taken pictures of other planets. Somehow we tend to think that we cannot get better at love and relationships. People like myself are even writing about it as you are reading right here. We repeatedly fail to apply a lesson that has already learned, and the cost of skin and tear that has already paid for it.

"We can learn to learn, or we can forever fail ourselves" ... N2P

What Have We Learned?"

I am going to list a few things that we know that does not work in a positive, loving relationship:

- Drug usage
- Seeing a married person
- Abusive behavior (without written consent)
- Lack of money
- Lack of housing
- Sharing all your business to the world
- Lacking the willingness to love better
- Outside drama

I could go on for days on the many subcategories under each of those listed above. Either we have seen this in our relationships or those friends and family; you can throw in the Jerry Springer show as well. The bottom line is, these items are at the core of most if not all dysfunctional relationships we have been a part of in the past or in right now.

"A valuable lesson is the one you only learned once" … N2P

Take a moment and jot down the lessons you have repeated and ask yourself, was it worth learning twice?

There are many things in my past that I have repeated; I am no different than anyone else. "However comma" I have learned to be more proactive in my relationships than reactive, which allows me to avoid most things that are relationship killers to the average relationship.

What I have learned:

- Ask more questions in the beginning
- If a person works multiple jobs, they have less time
- Drama does not magically appear, tadah!!
- Hurt people, hurt people.
- Applying what I learned makes me feel good
- A person's family tree is a factor
- Its ok to leave a bad situation

What have you learned?

Applying What We Learned

There are things we learned in our past relationships that we do not need to be in a relationship to develop a systematic way to apply the lessons learned. So, what do we do?

Quite often we hide in the house for years, saying the usual:

- Ain't no good men/women out there
- I'm going to wait on Jesus
- It's too much work
- I'm just going to raise my children
- I don't need a man/woman
- I give up

Why are you punishing yourself? The pain factor we go through while boosting our Relationship IQ is staggering, to say the least. But for some reason, we like to keep learning the old fashion way.

The key thing is practicing what we have learned already and build on it. Quite often we think we cannot apply relationship stuff without a relationship. I'm here to tell you can and should.

"The Art of Friendship" is just as important and allows you to practice everything you want to apply in your love relationship, minus sex.

What are the characteristics to a good friendship?

- Honesty
- Trust
- Communication
- Compatibility
- Common interests
- A need
- The willingness to work on it

What are the characteristics of a good relationship?

- Everything listed above
- Sex

We can practice all those characteristics with our friends and even coworkers. Best believe most horrible friends have horrible relationships. (I'll leave that right here)

I purposely practice on my relationship skills on everyone.

Example A:

I used to have issues expressing how I felt in a relationship. I would keep quiet and let it spew out like a volcano. This type of behavior is truly unhealthy for any relationship. I have learned to say how I feel to my friends. Because not everything they do is friend-like, why not start telling them how I feel. I began to share how I felt; some were receptive, and some were not. But the point is, I am practicing being able to do the same thing in a loving relationship without an emotional outburst.

If practice makes perfect, why are we not practicing on being better friends, which will make us better partners in relationships? If you cannot have a great relationship, at least you have better friendships.

Why do We Fail?

There are many reasons why we fail at connecting with the right person and sometimes stay with the wrong person:

- Old Pain
- Fear of new hurt
- Shame factor
- We are dumpable
- Angry at things cannot change (so we think)
- Emotionally numb

Those factors listed above are things we can control within ourselves because they are based on how we feel and deal with others. We fail because we lack the skills to do it better. We have a desire to feel our way through a relationship and not take a bird's eye view of what has been and what it could be.

The miracle in a relationship is only in the meeting, the rest of it is up to you and the other person. It seems the one who has been hurt the most and turned the negatives into positives has the higher Relationship IQ.

The higher the IQ, the calmer and readier a person will be for a positive lasting relationship.

Here lies the problem, I can tell you all that I have been through, all my bad and you will judge me by that. Thinking like that has become my norm. We say, "what doesn't kill us, makes us stronger," but we look at a person's past as a negative. After failing in many areas of relationships; I have an extremely high Relationship IQ. In Vol. 1 "Undumpable," I have taken a hard look at why my relationships ended and the roles I played in them. If I want a better and lasting relationship why not learn from where I failed as well as others?

Meeting and dating someone who has not learned from their past and is not attempting to do it better or smarter is unacceptable to me. If a person is not willing to be better at relationships, then they may have deeper issues. There are many ways to improve ourselves to be ready for "the one." We should want to want better in order to have better and conduct our walk in that manner.

Relationship Advice

I often hear people saying, "why would I want to take advice from someone who failed sevarval relationships; because the price of the lesson has already been paid.

The key thing you need to ask from those who have failed is:

- What was your decisionmaking factors
- How would you have done it differently?
- What was the lesson you learned?
- What was the outcome?

I am no longer in the business of repeating old lessons. I will ask many questions, generate new rules off the lessons learned by others to save my "life time." Because I believe in love, but I believe giving love a fighting chance from the start, not in the middle, and definitely not at the end. Ask yourself, are you using what you have learned?

Next Up:

Let's Make It work

Volume Five

Let's Make It Work

Preface

We are so shell shocked from the pain of failure from past relationships that we almost doom the next potential relationship before it gets to take flight. By now we have covered the selection and vetting process, understanding the concept of flags and whistles, and a general idea of how important it is to prepare yourself for the opportunity of meeting "The One."

You can have all the major tools in the box, but if you do not have the skills to complete the project, it will fail like the rest. So how can we make it work without going back to square one each time? All we have do is to find someone who wants peace in a loving relationship, just as bad as you do. Also, that person needs to have a "Relationship IQ" that is close to your own.

A Great Start

It all starts at hello, where it goes from there is the mystery. We want to make a great impression, and we want to be taken seriously. Our overall goal is to be in a happy, blissful relationship that has very little residue of our past failures. We have learned many lessons up to this point, and we do not want to relearn any of them if we can help it. All we need now is to find someone who we are evenly yoked with and is not emotionally damaged beyond self-repair.

We are stressed out so bad at this point we often ruin it really quick by saying a few of the following statements that yield a no callback:

- I'm dating with a purpose
- I'm not here to play any games
- If you anything like my ex
- I'm looking for a husband
- All I want is a wife to take care of me

We often talk our way right out of a good thing without even knowing it. Many of us have been fooled, misled, tricked, and let down so much that we want to set things straight right from the start. Quite often what is really going in the other person's ear is, "this person is "relationship thirsty." They are either running from or to something. This causes all kinds of unfounded flags to go up. When this happens, the listener is forced to make a very quick decision, which eight out ten times it is not in your favor.

The simple secret is to show the type of person you are in your walk. People can see husband and wife material in action. Ideally, people who want to be married would do better if they would conduct themselves as a married person. "However comma," just because you want to get married doesn't make you marriage material. If you want to be a doctor, you must go to the school of medicine. If you want to be a pilot, I think flight school is the place for you. Being a spouse is not something you should wish for, without the work. If you want to be in a relationship, you should practice being a friend. If you want a great start at a relationship; after you conquer loving yourself, then learn the ways of being what you want in your mate. If you want to be a side-chick/dude, talk to other side-pieces to make sure you are the best side-piece you can be. To be a functional husband or wife, speak with an array of married people to get the good, bad, and best practices. Hey, it's only for the rest of your life.

We need to have a realistic understanding of who we are in the food chain before we try to have more than we can handle, or settle for less than we deserve. Knowing who you are is three quarters of the battle. The last quarter is knowing how to see what you need to see in other people.

Who Are You?

We fall into three basic categories:

- Single Single
- Single Husband
- Single Wife

Single Single

The "single single" person is where we all start in the realm of relationships. We have no clue what it is to be a good friend and partner. We tend to function in a selfish manner and lack the awareness of the needs of others and what it takes to be in a serious committed relationship. Of course, we thought that when we were in the relationship of our lives in high school, but it was more of a yearning from our genitals than it was the concept of a true relationship. The closest thing to grasping the understanding was having that ride or die best friend. Being in a love relationship is pretty close to friendship, just minus the sex.

The Single Husband/Wife

These are divorced husbands and wives that are seeking to be in relationships or marriages again. They have (should have) an advanced understanding what is it like to be a partner.

Things like sharing, caring, compromising, and drawing up relationship goals should not be a stranger to them. If they did not do that in their marriage, there is a chance they have learned their lessons from their failures. I am a single husband; there are many things I know that must be carried out in the role of a husband. I have taken the time to work on the areas I felt I failed. When it comes to dating and the thought of being in a relationship, I find myself being drawn to a single wife.

I'm not saying that a single single person should not pursue a single husband/wife, but know that they are expecting someone seasoned in the art of a relationship and going back to square one could be hectic and time consuming, to say the least.

Making the Best of It

We cannot get around the understanding that this is a process. We would like to have "love at first sight" and live happily everafter, but that is so rare you might win the lotto first. "However comma" it doesn't mean that we should give up. No person besides those on death-row knows when their time is up. So why not just enjoy the journey of finding love. We have been fooled to think that love is the key, but we tend to skip one key element in a strong, lasting relationship, and that is friendship.

We are taught that putting people in the friend zone means they were not going to get a shot at the title. I think everyone needs to be in the friend zone first before you think of giving them an automatic upgrade to a love relationship. Friendships are very valuable and are the closest thing to a marriage. Ideally, you want to marry your best friend. If you live under the laws of being a good friend, there is a great chance you have what it takes to be a spouse. Take a moment and think about it, let it sink in. Most of you have friends and family members who are horrible friends and have horrible relationships, which is a nasty trend.

Learn to find joy in friendship, and you will have a better chance at having an emotionally fulfilled relationship.

Do Your Relationship Thing

I decided to change my relationship method of operation; which is how I approached and participate within a relationship. I said, from here on out, I will do things that make me feel good in my relationship. To include the following:

- Inspire growth in my partner
- Help with solving problems in their life
- Work on their vehicle
- Fix items around their home
- Model for their children
- Protect them

These are the things I wanted to do in a relationship, that I never had the emotional courage to carry out. I also understood that it would not be fair to me if I never get to do those things. I could no longer function under the idea that they may not be worthy of all I have to offer. When I came up with the idea, I was pretty much hiding in the house bouncing back from my divorce. I truly needed to know if I have what it took to be in a healthy relationship. Even more so, I desired the things

I didn't get to do in my marriage because I had no clue back then.

What I found out about myself was so powerful. I knew how to give, share, and care. My feet didn't feel like I had cement shoes stopping me from moving forward. I was expressing how I felt and loving it. This had nothing to do with the person. I mean, she was a great person, but I was doing my relationship thing. I can honestly say it did me some good.

Then I learned something else about the dating cycle. If you are doing positive things with a person, just being in your relationship mode, you get a snapshot of who they are in a relationship (of course if they are not in representative mode). Your positive actions should be contagious, and the other person should be happy to reciprocate. In other words, it will expose the other person's partnership skills. People can tell you all day what they think and want they will do in a relationship, but good people will get with the program. Those who have no clue will not know how to accept your positive relationship ways. How else do you measure who are dealing with without purposeful interaction?

What I was doing wrong was showing up and partially engaging in the relationship. I was trying to do the "hokie-pokie," I'd put my left foot in, and take my left foot out; that does not work in a relationship. When you play that game, you are constantly starting back a square one on a daily basis. You are not building on a positive yesterday, and nothing is gained. Your relationship thing is your participation within the relationship to get both of you to fertilize the relationship to grow as big as life. If two people are living and loving in fear, it is just a matter of time before it is corrupted with doubt and old pain.

If you never fully engaged in your relationship then you are hurting it. If your partner is not reciprocating, then this is just practice for the real relationship that is coming.

Find Peace in a Relationship

Let's start right here, stop telling each other that relationships require a lot of work as if it is more like a life sentence. Lazy people will never be in a worthwhile relationship. The relationship needs two people who want to be happy with each other. This means it will be what you make of it. Every word you use in the communication with that person has direct power over what you want at the end of the day.

Example:

A person who is not happy in their relationship may do the following:

- Call their mate out their name
- Not come home
- Have an affair
- Strike them
- Hide money
- Spend all the money

None of that breeds peace in a relationship, and at the end of the day, it says they do not want you. You cannot accept this in the gray matter between your ears any other way. People will have many different definitions of peace. Those items listed above do not come from a place of peace. My idea of relationship peace is two people, doing what they can in a loving manner to make sure that no external or internal chaos interrupts the euphoric feeling that is being generated through caring, sharing, compromising and consideration. This can only be accomplished by two people with the same relationship goals. Who doesn't want peace with their piece? People constantly tell you that, "no relationship is perfect." They have not tried; they often picked someone who was not worthy and put lipstick on a pig or a suit jacket on a monkey. The road to peace is paved with limitations, boundaries and realistic expectations to your relationship and they must be known. Not pay as you play, which most of us have been witness to for years. Now, of course, you know that you must have individual peace first before you can truly project it into a relationship. There are those who can fake it until they make it, I'm not mad at you at all. Remember peace is not our norm as a culture, and it is mildly disguised as boring, lame, and mundane, but this is mostly from the outside looking in.

When to End it

Let's breaks some eggs here. Unconditional love has conditions; we show it every day when we are forced to end a relationship. To tell the truth, I'm really scratching my head about Romeo and Juliet. That type of love needs to be reserved for parents and children. Anything else is truly over doing it. As we get older and begin to understand what is acceptable and what is not, the unconditional concept tends to fade. The realization that the person you thought loved as deep as you do is showing cracks in their relationship armor. You know the usual:

- Stop calling like they use
- Start staying away longer without explanation
- Lack of communication
- Goes into search mode (Bouncing Tyrone or Rent time Rita)
- Unexplained anger
- Missing in Action

These are few of the signs that your loving relationship is ending; many of us have been on the receiving end or have put them into play. In earlier days, we would beg and plead with people not to go, not to cut off that drug called love. I have created two life rules after being a victim of some of those embarrassing displays.

"Don't want nobody who doesn't want you" N2P

"Don't want something for someone else" N2P

Why would someone feel the need to create a rule? Because a lesson has been learned and there is no desire for you to repeat it. There are times we can see the end, and we know the feeling of rejection and pain. At this point of my life, I have created the power of the "walk away." My Relationship IQ says that this person no longer wants me. Therefore it is time for me to walk away. The desire to have closure is gone; no need for understanding why and can we work it out? I know a few are saying, wow that is cold. But when you find yourself begging into an empty phone and the only response you get is, "the caller's voicemail is full and is not accepting anymore more messages.... bye" a few times; then you haven't tasted the bitter ending of a relationship. When you can quietly notice that the other person lacks basic consideration of your feelings and forgoes the cardinal rules of engagement you both had agreed upon, then the end is very near my friend.

Suffering, neglect, abuse, and disrespect have nothing to do with love and having a positive and loving relationship. People tell other people that this is the natural flow of a love relationship. Our relationship dysfunction has become our norm and our personal acceptance of that norm from time to time has almost killed the loving spirit we have inside. This is why many of us tend to want to hide in religion and abstain from the physical joy of a relationship. The cost of getting it wrong is greater with each attempt.

When should you leave a relationship? When you feel, your partner has reached their maximum understanding of what a relationship is and has no desire to grow within the said relationship. I say this because we can learn to be better in relationships. There are books and other peoples' relationship isms and techniques to help move your relationship to the next level. The issue is, we tend to think that we do not want to do what someone else has done to better our relationship. But the art of the relationship is not new. Re-inventing the relationship wheel may not be in your partner's best interest.

"You ain't going to practice on me" N2P

As your Relationship IQ grows, you will be less tolerant of repeating the lessons you have already learned up to this point. This is a direct result of why our relationship time spans are getting shorter and shorter as we live longer and longer. When people says, they have zero tolerance, what they are really saying is, I used it all up in previous relationships. We do not run out of love; we tend to want to stop wasting the remaining love we have in us. Why put in it the hands of the unworthy? Unworthy is when you have learned many relationship lessons, and the other person only has a few under their belt.

Example:

I asked my woman on Thursday, "do you want to go out on Saturday?" She said, "no I have plans with my friends."

What should I do?

- A. Demand she change her plans
- B. Make her suffer for making plans with others
- C. Show up to where she is supposed to be
- D. Ask her out sooner than Thursday to make sure you can get the time slot.

I know for a fact in my younger days, I would not have been happy, and would probably take the whole scenario as a personal attack against my relationship; this is insecurity at its best. So, answer "A or B" would have been in play. "However comma" with a higher Relationship IQ, I developed the understanding that "D" would be far more effective and peaceful to my current relationship. I knew from my own history that "A and B" created more problems than it helped in the relationship. Answer "A and B" could very well be the grain of sand that could turn into a mountain of resentment and be a negative pivot point your relationship.

The end of a relationship is not the end of the world. Like in most Karate movies, you may have to seek a master to train you in the art, so you do not go out there and get your emotional ass kicked again. If you really want to make it work you have to know what you want at the end of the day and use everything you learned.

Next Up:

Sex

Preface

By now, I'm sure you have noticed that I have barely mentioned sex. That is because sex has a different meaning and use for everyone. I'm not here to tell you when to put sex is on the table, that is truly up to you and the person you have chosen. I'll say this; you get everything good with sex, as well as everything bad with it. What I will share are a few views you might have not openly spoken about that drug called sex.

The Game

I often hear the term, "people always playing games." The Game has various versions when it comes to sex; it is an age-old game of "catch a girl, get a girl." In our pre-teenage years, it was a natural exploration of our sexual urges and the fascination of the other sex. Eye-balling the neighbors and having those crazy internal feelings we use to have around certain people. That part of life is very natural and we cannot help how we are made. The problem is that we have become so civilized and doing what we naturally want to do is no longer acceptable. This portion of the game is not really a game, but it is life at its primal core.

Sex brings about the birth of children, and children bring about families, and they all bring about responsibilities. Where the game goes wrong is, at this stage most of our culture were not introduced to the full list of responsibilities and stressors of parenthood, even though this is how we came about. Being told sex is bad vs. the sensation in our groins has been a tough battle for decades. The constant struggle to educate and prepare our children not to repeat our journey is a milestone in a parent's life.

As a young boy, sex wasn't always on my mind; it was the heat of the summer that brought about the fire in me. I'm sure a few of you are nodding your head in remembrance of those days. Once I had my first taste of the forbidden fruits of life I was a player in the game. The game was to "get some" without getting caught. The wolf in the forest had nothing on me. I'd meet parents and go to churches; I had no shame in my game. The game didn't come with a coach; it was more of learn as you go. I couldn't tell anyone for years what I did with my "summer-time." The game became stronger and stronger, by the time I graduated from high school I was a father. The game had me caught up, and there was no turning back. Why? Because there was no one to stop me and explain the full concept of what I was doing or going through, nor the preparation of what might happen. Luckily for me, I had a plan where I was going to go after high school, and I stuck to it. The game I played with my life, is the same game that many are still doing today.

The Shame

The Shame of being in the game is that we take other people along for the ride with us. Those who had the same urges and a lack of full understanding of the ramification of their actions. I'm sure a few will think that their acrobatic motions were worthy of winning the gold in the Closet Sex Olympics, until the day you found yourself sitting on your momma's sofa and that damming sensation you had when you realized you just created another life.

The shame part should be that you had no forethought to what was about to take place for the next 20 years at a minimum. The Level of shame should be enough that you do not want to see this repeated in your new seed. Enough to want to put things in place to make sure that your children are better equipped for the game when it is their turn.

Shame on the parents who are aware of this and fail to attempt to prepare their child, knowing how hard it has been for you and the child you made while being a star player in the game. No shame in being human beings and doing what we do, but not evolving to make life easier for the children that are born from the game is sad.

The Drug

"Sex is not love; love is not sex... they are just cousins"..N2P

Sex is the self-medicating drug that would love to have a partner but can satisfy you when you are alone. We would go out in the greatest of storms, sacrifice our jobs, even risk the end of marriages and split up our families for that good good.

After we move pass the fascination phase of sex, we tend to find other uses for it:

- To control
- To manipulate
- To scheme
- To medicate
- To physically express love
- To substitute for real love

It took me well into my forties to figure out why I was substituting sex for real love. While other people turned to smoking weed, drinking until they pass out, to escape pain or some unwanted reality, sex became my drug of choice. I figured that those things were totally against my over goal in life. I also found out I was in search of love. It is hard to explain, but I came to the understanding that most of my life I was seeking the love of my mother and I was totally looking in the wrong direction. Life is about looking for your purpose and your rightful place, to include any missing pieces. Without proper guidance and love, we tend to be like lost sheep, and it is not until we are in the grip of the wolf's teeth we find that place or purpose.

Everyone has a reason for having sex, if you do not know by now, you need to take a time out and figure it out. Self-doping with sex is mentally unhealthy, and you tend to connect with the best sex, but not the right person. Sex is not love, because after you collapse, you still have the same issues, just like using any drug.

Life becomes peaceful once we know what we want, need, and do not need. I know that sounds easier said than done, but try it first before you think it is impossible.

Like with any drug, there a price. The cost varies from person to person, from never being capable of a serious relationship to scores of children to not having a full concept of what love is.

By no means am I saying sex is bad, it is one of the few joys on earth besides food and music. You cannot let sex lead you on your journey; it's just a natural part of our life that should never hold the map and compass.

The Love

As I said before, "sex is not love, love is not sex." When we get this twisted, we open ourselves up to a world of hurt. Yes, it is true you can have love without sex. People are fooled via the internet time and time again, by being emotionally duped into thinking they are in a loving relationship from hundreds, even thousands of miles away. Love is a feeling, that invades our logical thinking. Love is like a slippery lawyer that finds loop holes in our thinking process and then pleads the 5th. It knows what we want, that euphoric feeling that is better than any drug ever made. The only other drug that equals to that is sex.

If you really look at it, they both are really close cousins on the dysfunctional side of the family who function under the "by any means necessary clause." We cannot seem to live without them and when we do, its either through another drug or isolation from free thinking to abstain from them both.

When they are both utilized in the content of a positive and loving relationship, then you have the best life ever, worthy of envy and petty jealousy. We spend a good prtoin of our lives trying to bring the three into the most powerful triangle ever made.

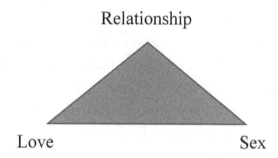

Relationship

Love   Sex

A relationship with just sex may work. Sex without a love may work as well. Love without a relationship breeds a lot of limitations. Sex can function solo, but that leads to a lonely existence of always seeking the next partner. Two people can function with one or two items not present. Quite often if someone is settling for two of the three, there could very well be some deep scarring that has not been uncovered…. yet.

It would really help if we had our own definition of love and an understanding of why we have sex. This should be a part of getting to know someone phase. We often do not know the "whys" and later find out during the break-up stage of a relationship. Quite often we are not brave enough to share what those things mean to us. Or so hurt we try to deny ourselves one or two points of the triangle all together.

As we evolve, we should be better at many things to include relationships. Self-love has to be high on our "must-have" list. This will pave the way to having a complete triangle, and we would have a greater chance of having a positive, loving relationship, that we often read about in books. In our pursuit for the triangle we will fail many times and kiss a lot of frogs and frogettes, but many do not give up, and that is what love wants.

Last Call

As I stated before there is no exact science to finding the perfect mate, but not trying to make since of the search for love is foolish and dangerous, because it requires other people. Most of our greatest highs and deepest pains comes via the pursuit of "The One." The one is that person that was made so perfect for you and it will test you to break all your rules. Therefore, you need to prepare yourself and strive to be undumpable when that person comes into your life.

Search for a friend and you just might find "The One".... N2P

Read you Later........